Panorama-Books: S P A I N

30 photos in colours

W. KUDRNOFSKY

SPAIN

MÜNCHEN - WIEN

WILHELM ANDERMANN VERLAG

Wrapper and cover designed by Gerhard M. Hotop

Translated by D. Kempff

U.S. and Canadian Distributors

FRENCH & EUROPEAN PUPLICATIONS Inc.

Rockefeller Center, New York, N.Y.

48793

© 1957 by Wilhelm Andermann Verlag, Munich. All rights reserved by the publisher.

Printed in Germany. 259

SPAIN

Beyond that southern line where the earth of the European continent is thrust up to form the last frontier mountain range lies Spain, a land seemingly predestined by geography to serve as Europe's antechamber but which, when beauty of scenery and wealth of historical monuments are considered, is really its most sumptuous state-room. Spain's past was even more eventful than that of the rest of Europe and has left more numerous and more highly-coloured traces. These, combined with the natural beauties of the country, call forth some of the most wonderful impressions that a traveller can take back from the Old World.

Spain is attached to Europe by a relatively narrow land bridge. The frontier wall of the Pyrenees was an additional factor militating against relations with continental Europe, and thus Spain is entirely turned towards the sea. It is true that another Mediterranean country, Italy, is in a similar situation, but the results are different in the two cases. The leg of the Italian boot extends too far into Europe for it to have been possible for the country's historical destinies ever to be independent of those of her northern neighbours. Moreover, the foot stretches into the blue waters of the South and the opposite coastline is far away. The South of Spain, on the contrary, the most beautiful part of the country, is so close to another continent that numerous formative influences on Spanish history inevitably emanated from across the narrow straits. The short distance between Tarifa and Ceuta – only ten kilometres – was an important factor in the foundation of a centuries-old African past on Spanish soil.

True this short sea crossing between Africa and Spain was not only used in the northerly direction. When history was pleased to call stronger peoples into play against the North African intruders, the latter had to leave Spain by the same way they had come. Since the year 1100 B.C., when the Phoenicians founded their settlements Cadiz and Tartessos in southern Spain, there has always been in the Straits of Gibraltar a lively maritime traffic which has played a vital rôle in shaping the destinies of all who participated in it.

Thus, by reason of this close proximity to the great African continent, Spain has ever been a coveted object for the power which happened to control that soil. However, when the Phoenicians crossed from Africa into Europe on the first occasion in historical times, the ambitions of the individual tribes were much less mutually exclusive than they later became. The Iberians, who were already settled in the eastern coastal regions at the period for which we possess the first historical evidences, were not driven out by the Phoenicians but respected as neighbours. In the sixth century B. C., when the Celts came streaming into Spain from the North there was no fighting, only peaceful mixing. From then on the new tribe of Celt-iberians inhabited the district of present-day Barcelona.

Spain had room for many people, and even at that time Nature abhorred a vacuum. For two centuries the Phoenicians spread over western Spain also, and the domination of Africa over European soil continued to extend. After the first Punic War, Spain became an African colony (almost exactly 2 000 years later, the opposite phenomenon was to occur, at least in part). Hannibal created a Carthaginian empire, successor of the Phoenician vanguard, on the wide spaces between the rivers Ebro and Tagus, and Hasdrubal built a lasting monument to this period in 221 B.C., when he founded New Carthage, the modern Cartagena.

But the Carthaginians were not destined to hold Spain for long. After thirty years of rule they were driven out by Scipio Africanus the Elder. The First Punic War had opened Spain to the Carthaginians. In the Second, they lost it again.

The course of Spanish history was now guided for many centuries by the flourishing Roman power, but it was no straight course. As the Urbs was shaken by repeated internecine power struggles, the provinces and colonies were drawn into these quarrels by the jealousies of governors and proconsuls, to the detriment of their peaceful development. A century after the Roman conquest, the country was split into two warring halves: Hispania citerior under the rebel praetor Sertorius against Hispania ulterior commanded by the Roman general Sulla. It was only in 45 B.C. that Julius Caesar finally succeeded in establishing his authority over what was to become the Roman Empire. Sertorius' troops capitulated and the whole of Spain was incorporated into the world empire of Augustus. But Spain was no Roman colony. Her population enjoyed the protection of Roman civil law, her poets – Seneca, Lucan, Martial – were fêted as Latin poets, and three of her sons, the Emperors Trajan, Hadrian and Theodosius the Great, were called from their native land to guide the destinies of Rome.

It was only the disintegration of the Roman Empire four centuries later which made extensive changes possible. The great migration of peoples brought numerous tribes from Central Europe to the coastal regions of Spain. The Vandals settled in the South, the Alans in Portugal, the Suevi in the Northeast, while the Visigoth made their home in the territory which is now Barcelona.

But freedom from Roman rule was paid for by a long succession of wars. The tribes began struggles among themselves which were to last three centuries and in which we can already discern the characteristics of wars of religion.

Once again it was the close proximity of Africa which gave a turn to events destined to determine the development of the next great chapter of Spanish history. In order to defend themselves against Roderich, King of the Visigoths, his enemies concluded an alliance with the Moors of North Africa. In 711, battle was joined at Jerez de la Frontera between Roderich's troops and the North Africans. The Goths were defeated and Jerez de la Frontera became the bridgehead for a Moorish invasion of Europe as important in its far-reaching effects as the happenings of our own day. During the two centuries which their victorious progression lasted, armies of Arabs and Mahommedan Berbers occupied the whole southern coast. The capital of the Visigoths, "Barcinona" was conquered, its Gothic name changed to "Bardschaluna" and thus brought nearer to the present Barcelona. And when, finally, the Pyrenees were reached without the fighting force of the Africans having been spent, Gaul became the next objective. In 717 Moorish troops took Narbonne and Lyons, and it was only forty years later that they were finally driven from France.

The Moorish domination over the greater part of the Iberian peninsula was to last much longer. It is true that the Moors did not succeed, despite their unique succession of victories, in conquering the whole territory which today constitutes Spain. The northern coast and the Basque provinces remained in the possession of the Goths. Nevertheless, the marks of their centuries of occupation are so numerous that they dominate the impressions of Spain which the present-day traveller brings back.

The city from which the Moors exercised their rule was Cordova – that "Corduba" which, a century and a half before the Christian era, had enjoyed a privileged position as capital of the Roman province of Hispania ulterior. It was now the capital of the new Spanish Caliphate, with all the further advantages such a position implied. As a cultural centre of the Moslem world, it became the European Mecca, attracting students from all over the West in search of knowledge of the new doctrine of Islam.

Before the Moors occupied the country, Christianity had already spread over great areas of Spain. But now that the Oriental religion of Islam had entered the land with the new rulers, it seemed as though there could be no future for the Christian faith. However, the Moors, occupied above all in extending and consolidating their new empire, showed themselves tolerant. The exercise of the Christian religion was not persecuted but everywhere permitted. Daily contact with the foreign conquerors was, however, not without consequences; the Christians in the occupied parts of the country learned the Arab tongue and gradually adopted Arab habits of life.

The most flourishing period of the Moorish empire was towards the end of the first millenium A. D. After Charlemagne's war against the Moors had ended in final

9

defeat at Roncevaux and Count Roland, leader of the imperial armies, had been killed, the real period of Moorish domination began. The Amirate under the Omayyads was followed in 929 by the Caliphate of Cordova. A year later the new ruler Abdurrahmân III succeeded in occupying the still independent state of Toledo.

Soon, however, the mighty empire of the Moors began to show the first evidences of decline. At first, it was only a matter of a few lost battles – a purely external sign. Then, in 1030, when the last Omayyad Caliph, Hischâm III, abdicated and the unity of the central government came to an end, the decay began to attack the very roots of Moorish power. Once again a great empire was shaken by dissensions, but this time the disunity was not to be the prelude to a restoration, as in the days when the rebellious Roman leader Sertorius was vanquished by Sulla, but to the blow which brought the whole Moorish empire crumbling to dust.

The temporary union of states previously divided by the strong rivalries of individual tribal leaders which was carried through by the Berber sect of the Almoravides could only retard, but not halt, the southern advance of Christian rule. In addition, the military power of the Moors was greatly weakened by the necessity of putting down numerous revolts in their homeland. Five hundred years after the Caliph of Damascus had declared Spain a Moorish province, the Kingdom of Granada was all that remained of the Arab possessions in Europe, which had been raised in the course of the intervening centuries to the rank of an independent Caliphate. All the rest had been lost to the growing strength of the Catholic kings. On 1st January 1492, Abu Abd'allah Mahomed XIII, the last Moorish ruler in Europe, had to leave Spain. Four years earlier he had lost Malaga in battle against the

Christians. From that time onwards the whole country was in the possession of European princely and royal houses.

The foundation of the new Christian state – the Reconquista – had its beginnings in the northern coastal regions. Since Moorish rule even at the time of its greatest territorial extension had never reached the north coast, the old spirit – which was to be the spirit of the new Spain – was free to prepare the Reconquest unhindered. It was in the Basque province of Navarra and the neighbouring Asturias that the forces of the new state were based. In 801 Louis the Pious succeeded in making good the failure of his father Charlemagne at Roncevaux by winning from the Arabs the independent "Spanish March" of Barcelona. He thus cut the enemy off from access to the Pyrenees and created the most important military stronghold in the North of the country. The new Kingdom of Castile, consisting of the provinces of Castile, Navarra and Aragon, was now for long the centre of resistance. In 1094, at the head of his army of mercenaries, the "Cid" (Arabic Sidi = Chief) Rodrigo Diaz de Vivar, who is still the national hero of Spain, conquered Valencia on his own initiative and thus enriched Castile by another province.

The following centuries saw the spread of the new Christian power in the North and the unification of provinces still isolated. The separation of Portugal, whose history had been concomitant with that of Spain, falls into this period at the end of which Castile, linked with the northwestern province of Leon, reached in an unbroken circle over the whole north coast and down to the Mediterranean.

Henceforth only Granada and the south coast proper remained in Moorish hands, but when, in 1236, Cordova, the spiritual centre of Islam on European soil, and, twelve years later, Seville, fell to the Christian troops, the Moorish power was broken for ever.

Contemporaneously with the final consolidation of Christian rule and national unity, an event occurred of immense importance for the future of all Europe, but in the first instance, for the further development of Spain – the discovery of America by Christopher Columbus who, on 3rd August 1492 – the year of the fall of Granada – began his journey with three sailing ships from the harbour of Paolo de la Frontera near Huelva. Although Columbus was an Italian, his discovery is considered a Spanish achievement, for the ships he used and the financial backing of the enterprise were Spanish (the annual Fiestas in Spain are held, moreover, to celebrate this event).

Spain, which had been almost extinguished as a state in Europe during the period of Moorish domination, now rapidly developed into a world power with a greatness she was never again destined to achieve. This resulted not least from the fact that the internal struggles of the various kingdoms and of the nobles against each other ceased and Spain was united for the first time under her present name by "His Catholic Majesty" King Ferdinand of Aragon and Queen Isabella the Catholic of Castile.

The discovery of America by Columbus led to the foundation of the Spanish colonial empire. The new tasks which this involved for Spain diverted her attention from what had been the first aim of the united kingdom – the colonisation of North Africa – and this certainly to the advantage of Spain, for, if we remember that Spanish is today spoken by nearly 100 million people in South and Central

America, Mexico and the Philippines, making it the most widely used language after English, it is easy to see the lasting fruits which the policy of those days has borne.

The 16th century saw the exploitation of all the newly-discovered territories by absolute monarchs whose collaboration with the Catholic Church – which had also become a strong power – has left its mark in many a monument of interest and delight to the present-day visitor. Thanks to a wise policy of marriage and succession, the ruling Hapsburg house was able to strengthen and consolidate its position until Spain reached the peak of her fortunes under Charles I, who was crowned Emperor of the Holy Roman Empire. But it proved to be impossible for his successor Charles V to keep in his hands all the reins of the mighty Spanish state. Under Philip II, the seven Netherlands Provinces, aided by Protestant England – the strongest rival of Catholic Spain – broke away. The war began in 1585; three years later the Spanish Armada was destroyed off the coast of England and the fate of the world empire of Spain sealed.

The day of a change of leadership had dawned in Europe. While England and the Netherlands replaced Spain on the seas, and thus became a permanent threat to her colonial possessions, France took over the leading rôle on the Continent.

The 17th century brought nothing but losses to Spain. The wars with France emptied the coffers of the state without bringing any gains. By the Treaties of Westphalia the Netherlands recovered their independence. Portugal, which had temporarily come under the Hapsburg crown, was also lost.

The 18th century opened with the loss of the War of Spanish Succession which cost Spain her last European possessions: Belgium, Milan and Southern Italy. Even

parts of the Spanish motherland, Gibraltar and Mallorca, came into British possession. The war which Philip V, in desperation, began against Austria ended with
Spain being forced, by the Treaty of the Hague, to return the few conquests which
this campaign had brought her.

The change in ruling families when Philip V, the first Bourbon, succeeded to the
Habsburgs had thus not set a term to the decline of the former world empire. In
addition to her setbacks on the European continent, Spain was now to suffer the
loss of her colonies. As the ally of Napoleon she once again lost practically her
whole fleet in a naval battle with the English at a time when rebellion was threat-
ening in North America. By 1825, i.e., twenty years after Trafalgar, all the colonies
on the American continent from Argentina to Mexico had thrown off the rule of
the motherland. Apart from unimportant enclaves in Africa, the only overseas
possessions remaining were the West Indian islands Cuba and Puerto Rico and the
Philippines. In 1898, Spain finally lost these last remnants of her former world
power.

What strength Spain still retained at the beginning of the 19th century was
gradually exhausted in civil wars fought to decide the rival claims of kings or their
successors. First came the quarrel of the regency of Ferdinand VII, who suspended
the Constitution and was afterwards compelled to restore it. There followed the
Carlist rebellion provoked by the supporters of Don Carlos against Isabella II.
This was followed by the constitutional struggles which led to the expulsion from
the country of Isabella II. In none of these contests was there any real victor –
unless the triumph of disunion over reason can be reckoned a victory.

When, in 1873, in keeping with the tendency of the times, the Republic, which would have been the only means of putting an end to these petty quarrels, was proclaimed, opponents immediately arose and a year later they succeeded in reversing the decisions of the Cortes. Once again the Carlists entered the scene and bloody struggles ensued. But Fortune had finally deserted the Carlist banners. In 1874, Alphonso XII became king and two years later Don Carlos left Spain for ever.

In 1886, a year after the death of King Alphonso XII, his son Alphonso XIII, still a child, was formally proclaimed king. His mother took over the Regency until he was declared of age. But in her hands the former world empire shrank still further. During the war with the United States in 1898, Spain saw her fleet annihilated for the third time and suffered the loss of her last colonies.

The 20th century began with certain more auspicious signs for Spain. Having realized their ambitions for autonomy, the states of Central and South America were suddenly conscious of their love for their former motherland. Thus, a "Pan-Iberian Movement" was founded. But this ideological gain could not offset Spain's economic losses, and so her interest turned towards Morocco. However, the campaign of 1909 against the Kabyles of the Rif brought no clear decision and, in the same year, an anarchist uprising took place in Barcelona. The working-class mob, angered by the costly and bloody Moroccan campaign, set fire to churches and monasteries. The rising was indeed quelled, but that did not put an end to popular discontent. Tens of thousands now began to leave a country fallen upon evil days to settle in America.

After the first world war, in which exhausted Spain had managed to remain neutral, there were further revolts. Once again it was the losses in Morocco which finally unleashed discontent with the government. This time Alphonso XIII's reaction was even more radical. He entrusted Captain-General Primo de Rivera in Barcelona with the establishment of a military dictatorship. But seven years later as the general had not succeeded in bringing about a lessening of social tensions, he forced him to resign. In the following year, 1932, Alphonso XIII himself had to abdicate. Once again the Republic was proclaimed in Madrid.

The succeeding years saw the preparations for the great Spanish Civil War which was to cost the country over a million dead. This struggle could have served as a warning to the other countries of Europe, but in 1939, the year in which the struggle ended in Spain, Europe declared war on herself.

Once again Spain succeeded in keeping out of the international conflict. Since that time all her efforts have been bent on retaining her remaining possessions, and in this she has followed the only path now possible for a European nation.

Whereas political history always seems to be played out with an eye to future consequences, happenings in the field of the history of art have no other purpose than to seize and hold the attention of the spectator in the present. But although artistic creation is so consciously indifferent to the future it is precisely this future which profits most from it. If we had only the reports of chroniclers at our disposal our knowledge of the lives of our forefathers would be incomplete – we would know nothing of their inner emotions. Only the reality of a thousand year-old

Ampurias

Cadaqués

*Barcelona. Aveni
de Rivera*

*Barcelona. The A
Primo de Rivera*

*Barcelone. Avenu
de Rivera*

...rcelona. Kathedrale
...rcelona. The Cathedral
... cathédrale de Barcelone

Aussicht vom Tibidabo
View from the Tibidabo
Vue de Tibidabo

Montserrat

Valencia.
Torreos de Serrano
Valence.
Torreos de Serrano

encia. Seidenbörse
encia. Silk Market
ence. La Bourse de la soie

Punta Ifach
La pointe d'Ifach

Elche. Palmenwald
Elche. The palm trees fo
Elche. La Palmeraie

Granada. Blick auf die Alhambra und Generalife
Granada. View of Alhambra and the Generalife
Grenade. Vue de l'Alhambra et du Généralife

Löwenhof

The Court of

La cour des lions

Granada. Generalife
Granada. The Generalife p
Grenade. Le Généralife

Sevilla. Alkazar und Kathedrale
Sevilla. The Alcazar and the Cathedral
Séville. L'Alcazar et Cathédrale

Sevilla. Alkazar, Mädchenho⟨⟩
Sevilla. The Alcazar, Court ⟨⟩
young girls
Séville. L'Alcazar, cour des
jeunes filles

Stierkampf in Sevilla
Bull fight in Sevilla
Corrida à Séville

Córdoba. Kathedrale
Córdoba. The Cathedral
Cordoue. La cathédrale

Córdoba. Kathedrale
Córdoba. Interior of the
cathedral
Cordoue. Vue de l'intérieur
de la cathédrale

Madrid. Puerta del Sol

Madrid. Edificio España

Madrid. Prado

Landschaft bei Toledo
Landscape near Toledo
Le paysage près de Tolède

Toledo. Puerta del Sol
Tolède. Puerta del Sol

Segovia. Aquädukt
Segovia. The aqueduct
Ségovie. L'aqueduc

Segovia. Alkazar
Segovia. The Alcazar
Ségovie. L'Alcazar

thedral, of a pre-historic cave drawing, or of a play from another century fills
, during our journey into the past, with understanding for what gave the men of
sterday, or the day before yesterday, the strength to endure the trials of life and
lls us what they welcomed as beautiful or rejected as ugly.

For the foreign guest in search of such discoveries, Spain is one of the most
tonishingly rewarding of all countries. In the course of his journey he finds the
ving evidence for everything which he has previously learned from historical
port. Even when, under a foreign sky and far from all monuments, he meets a
ing very much of the present – a Spanish peasant, or the same peasant's child on
e way to school – he is overcome by the feeling that the past has played a magi-
an's trick and confronts him, alive and real, in the present.

And yet Spain is not a museum, even in those places where for a modest sum she
veals her treasures under that title. The visitor contemplating a Greco or a
urillo in the Prado in Madrid, for instance, is not only conscious of the finished
nd created work, but often has the impression that he sees the artist himself as he
ainted, and it seems to him that he can experience in his mind and heart what it
as that led the master to use his brush exactly so and not otherwise.

This eloquence is, however, only the projection of a will to draw the beholder
to the current of creative force. The latter stands in the presence of the work of
t which has united in itself the inexhaustible stream of creative power. If he res-
onds to it, he is immediately overpowered and begins suddenly to see more than
he surface representation. He looks behind the creation and recognizes the sources
rom which content and form have emerged.

Such an intuitive reconstruction of the past naturally presupposes the presence of numerous and varied traces of earlier centuries, and in Spain particularly these are not lacking. Indeed, they reach back far into pre-historic times. Thus, on the roof of the Altamira cave on the north coast we find the beautifully proportioned representation of a buffalo painted with great economy of effect by an Aurignac man in Paleolithic times. Such witnesses to the earliest periods of human life are naturally rare, although there are caves on the south coast with paintings over 20 000 years old and already showing signs of North African influences.

There are also remains – it is true generally in ruins and decayed by wind and weather – of the days when Spain was first colonised by the peoples of the great empires of Antiquity. We need only mention the former Greek Emporion in Ampurias from the soil of which foundations of a whole quarter of the city were dug, and Cadiz, where the Phoenicians stored their treasures of tin and silver and where many finds from their necropolis are to be seen in the local archeological museum. However, the lion's share in these early remains belongs to the Romans whose walls even today are often included in the planning of city boundaries. A marvellous juxtaposition of Iberian, Carthaginian and Roman building can be seen in Sagunto on the south coast. The "Castillo" is mainly Arab, but is constructed on foundations dating from earlier epochs.

The three centuries of domination by the Visigoths, on the other hand, have left their traces mainly in the history of artisanal work. The crowns of the Visigoth kings are among the most beautiful examples of the goldsmith's art ever produced. It is in the North, where the rule of the Visigoths continued longest, that the most

48

gnificant example of their architecture is to be found in the shape of the former
Gothic royal hall of the 9th century near Oviedo which today serves as the church
of "Santa Maria de Naranco". The strange representation of the Virgin and Child
known as "Virgin de la Oca" which is said to date from the 7th century is preserved
in Burgos Cathedral.

The artistic life of Spain experienced a mighty upsurge with the beginning of the
Saracen domination. When the Arabs set foot on the European continent in
711 A. D., they brought with them, in addition to their foreign faith, the knowledge
of a highly-developed architecture. The harmonious combination of Arabic influences – which included a feeling for luxuriant ornamentation – found expression
in the splendid buildings which the traveller unconsciously associates with idea
of Spain.

The Moors excelled in rich ornamental work and, since the Islamic religion forbade
representations of Nature, this talent found its expression in architectural and
artisanal forms. Their architecture is unique. As one of the most beautiful examples
the "Mesquita" in Cordova, the capital of the Moorish Caliphate, merits special
mention. It was begun in 785 and provisionally terminated in the 10th century.
Today it is still one of the largest mosques in the world. 856 independent columns
support the roof, which is barely twelve metres high and through which the rare
daylight filters into the interior of the building. The obscurity in which this forest
of columns is always bathed at first awakens in the beholder a feeling of baffling
infinity, and it is only later that he succeeds in forming a general idea of the marvellous edifice. Unfortunately, the advance of the Christian religion after the Reconquest

did not spare the interior of the mosque. In the 16th century, 63 columns were removed from the centre to provide room for the building of the "Coro", a Christian church in the middle of the monument to Islamic art. The unity of the forest of columns (some original elements of which are thought to have come from more ancient buildings) was destroyed in favour of a building which would have enjoyed the advantage of much greater accessibility had it been erected elsewhere. The mosque, which is 179 metres long and 129 metres wide, was surrounded by a wall – in places 20 metres high – the crenellation of which lends to the whole the appearance of a fortress. A third of the total surface is occupied by the courtyard, where the trees are watered by means of a network of very narrow channels running between the flagstones. This is a type of canalisation found in all places where the Moors – a people from the desert regions of North Africa – erected their buildings. Near the main entrance to the courtyard, the 60 metre-high bell tower or "Campanario" was built in the 16th century. On its pinnacle is the statue of the Archangel Raphael, patron saint of the city of Cordova.

Another building which is if possible an even more noble monument to the architectural skill of the Arabs, is the "Palacio arabe de la Alhambra", built in the 14th century on the Monte Mauror in Granada as residence for the Moorish rulers. The legendary origin of the Arab name for the castle "Medînat al-ambrâ" (the red city) is as follows: the Moorish soldiers who were carrying out the building had to fight by day and had only the night in which to work. The whole building was bathed in a red light from the flame of their torches and at a distance it seemed as though a "red city" were being built.

The plan of this "red city" is a perfect example of the Islamic art of palace building. The inside of the Alhambra is divided into three principal parts: the "Mexuar" reserved for the exercise by the ruler of government busines, the Divan – the royal palace proper – and the Harem, the women's apartments. In each of these divisions the rooms give on to a central courtyard – the Myrtle court in the case of the Divan, and the Lion court in that of the Harem. The rooms of this palace are of medium size, and, in order to keep out the hot sun as much as possible, are provided with relatively small arched windows from which there is a splendid view over the city of Granada, several hundred metres below. The decoration of the rooms is unique in its splendour; the walls are covered over and with arabesques, and artistic and airily cut stalactites hang from the vaults above the entrance. The network of canalisations carries an unending stream of cooling water through courts and gardens to nourish the cypresses and orange trees. Two centuries after the Moors had completed their building, Charles V enlarged the Alhambra by erecting near the palace of the Mahommedan rulers his own palace which bears his name. Although it was never quite finished, it is a wonderful example of Spanish High Renaissance. Among other things, this palace was provided with a bullring of about 30 metres diameter in which the caballeros exercised themselves in the use of arms against bulls in a far more dangerous way than is usual today.

On the precipice of Cerro del Sol near the Alhambra is the "Palacio del Generalife". This edifice was finished some seventy years before work was completed on the Alhambra and served the Moorish kings as a summer residence. It is considerably smaller than its neighbour to the West and its greatest beauty is its splendid park which, with its grottoes and terraces, its fountains and hedges trimmed with geometrical precision, is a most beautiful example of Arab garden architecture.

The other monuments of Moorish architecture in Spain are of lesser importance although they too largely determine the character of the surrounding city or countryside. Mention should be made of the Mudejar style, a combination of Moorish with medieval Christian architecture. The 14th century Alcazar of Seville is a good example of this manner of building.

What the Moorish style was for southern Spain, the Romanesque which, with its characteristic barrel vaulting, penetrated from France in the 11th century, was for the Northwest. The cathedral and shrine of Santiago de Compostella, the pilgrimage church in the province of Galicia, the southwest tip of Europe, served as a model for many other cathedrals and churches in Spain which are built on the same basic plan. The churches in Avila and Segovia are examples.

The following centuries saw the spread of Romanesque to the South and East as far as the province of Catalonia. Above all, however, there now began a change of emphasis from the purely architectonic to the plastic and pictorial. Most of the frescoes of this period can be seen today only in the Barcelona Museum, but there are still sufficient examples of Romanesque sculpture in the churches themselves, above all on the richly-decorated capitals of the supporting columns.

The Gothic style which now came to flower was the first to conquer the whole Iberian peninsula – but with a strong admixture of the earlier modes. The Mudejar style already mentioned was the first of these combinations of Arab and Gothic elements ("mudëjelat" in Arabic is "subjected", and the term was applied to the

Moors as the conquered race). At the end of the Gothic period it was above all the Plateresque style which as the characteristic combination ("platero" means silversmith), for the early Renaissance, with its emphasis on the plastic, was beginning to luxuriate on the Gothic buildings, creating decorative elements in stone which resemble the fine work of the silversmith.

In the meantime, however, Gothic was also developing in its pure form. At the beginning of the 13th century, the cathedrals of Burgos, Toledo and Leon – the supreme examples of the French style in Spain – were erected. A subsequent development particular to Spain is the church with the "Coro" in the nave, enclosed within wide walls which create unusual spatial relationships. An earlier example of this existed, nevertheless, in Burgos cathedral.

The plastic and pictorial arts were now slowly beginning to free themselves from architecture and thus from the religious themes which they had cultivated almost exclusively. They were ceasing to be the handmaids of the Church and beginning to serve the secular power of kings and princes. In the first instance, the Spanish painters modeled themselves on the Italians, later, on the Dutch who, as soon as they came to Spain, settled principally in Castile.

While the Renaissance was spreading over Europe, the world power of Spain was growing to the peak of its prosperity. But the development of indigenous Spanish painting was at that time only in its infancy. In this respect, Spain began to catch up with her neighbours only after her material decline had already set in. The Greek Domenico Theotokopuli – el Greco – laid the foundations of the universal renown of Spanish art towards the end of the 16th century, but Spain only began

to have a school of her own in the 17th century. The founder was Francisco Ribalta in Valencia. His most important disciple is considered to be Juisepe de Ribera. Ribera himself, when he had reached the age of the teacher, finally succeeded in gathering around him a group of disciples whose names are associated with the golden age of Spanish painting: Zurbaràn, Cano, Velàsquez and Murillo. He who would gain an idea of the "Spanish School", its structure and its representatives, should not fail to visit the Prado in Madrid. No other museum in the world contains richer collections of important works of art all from the hands of painters of a single nation. The student of the works of individual Spanish masters – Velàsquez, for instance, who is represented here by more than fifty canvases, including his greatest "The Court Ladies" and "The Tapestry-weavers", has no choice but to begin his studies in the Prado.

Among the plastic and pictorial arts in Spain, painting alone attained a style of its own, worthy to serve as universal example. It was only towards the end of the Renaissance that sculpture produced anything of note. The early Baroque period was its high summer, and this is easily explained by the Spanish love for exuberant ornament and sumptuous decoration (constantly rekindled by the spectacle of the monuments of the Moorish epoch) which found in Baroque innumerable occasions to express itself. That these tendencies often led to excesses and bad taste – such as the use of set-in jewelled eyes and real hair to make figures more "natural" – was in the very nature of Baroque. Fortunately, architectural sculpture escaped these excesses, and thanks to the two great Baroque sculptors, Hernàndes and Montanes, the transition to the styles of a later period was successful.

On the whole, developments in architecture can be said to have followed general European trends, although the repeated signs of a quest for a specifically national form should not be overlooked. In this respect, a particularly striking example is furnished by the "Templo de la Sagrada Familia" in Barcelona, begun in the present century and not yet completed. The neo-Catalonian style of this church, which is somewhat reminiscent of Gothic models, contains essentially new elements.

Nevertheless, in the 20th century, it is once again through the medium of painting that Spain exercises a formative influence beyond the Pyrenees and Atlantic. Modern painting draws its principal spiritual substance from the Spaniard Picasso, for it was he who set off the chain-reaction which has taken place in the development of styles in our time. Thus, through her son Pablo Picasso, living in France, Spain has once again conquered the world.

Ampurias

Another Greek foundation is Ampurias, the port of Emporion of Antiquity. It is thanks to the solid Greek construction that the harbour mole, built of heavy stone blocks, is still today fulfilling its original purpose. Near the beach extends the site of the ancient port proper, levelled to the earth, however, by the ravages of time, so that today only the flat outline of the foundations bears witness to the fact that before the dawn of our era a people lived here whose sense for symmetry and order was applied equally to the Cosmos and to the material arrangements of everyday life on earth.

Cadaques

Cadaques is typical of these small fisher villages which lend ever-present animation to the natural beauty of this roughly two hundred kilometre-long ribbon of coast. But the foundations on which the present inhabitants of Costa Brava built were laid by the representatives of a rich culture, now extinct, but which once extended to the furthest reaches of the Mediterranean; about two thousand five hundred years ago the sea-faring Greeks discovered and settled this charming part of Spain. The name of Cape Aphrodisium, near Cadaques, remains as a memento of those distant days.

Costa Brava approaching Llansà

He who enters Spain via Port Bou receives at the very beginning of his journey a never-to-be-forgotten gift as a token of welcome: the experience of the "Costa Brava". Time after time the road drops down to the sea and to the many small fisher villages whose picturesque situation lends to this so-called "wild coast" an extremely peaceful and contemplative character. That impression of international tourist routine and of luxury grown rather stale which the traveller often feels on the Riviera is happily entirely absent on this part of the Mediterranean coast. The Costa Brava is a piece of genuine Nature, like the people who inhabit it.

Barcelona. Avenida Primo de Rivera

After the quiet atmosphere of the Costa Brava, which has taken him somewhat out of Time, the traveller soon becomes conscious of the present when he reaches Barcelona. The activity of this city of two million inhabitants meets him the moment he crosses the municipal boundaries and inreases in intensity the closer he comes to the centre, the Plaza de Cataluña. Although the origins of the Catalonian capital stretch far back into the past, the city we see today is a modern creation. High buildings in the American style which date from the beginning of the present century house the offices of companies whose economic relations with the New World are numerous and varied.

Barcelona. The Cathedral

On the highest point of the Old City of Barcelona, Mount Tabor, the cathedral of Santa Eulalia (also known as Santa Cruz) was built in the 13th century. On the north-east door can still be seen a few stone reliefs from the Romanesque edifice which formerly stood on this site. Work on the cathedral continued into our century and was terminated in 1913 with the erection of the domed tower.

View from Tibidabo

No visit to Barcelona would be complete without an excursion to Tibidabo, the five hundred metre-high lookout on the edge of the city, from which in clear weather the view of Barcelona and the sea is equally splendid by night and day. The Balearic Islands, two hundred kilometres distant, can be seen quite clearly.

Montserrat

In an isolated situation about sixty kilometres inland from Barcelona on the road to Saragossa, Montserrat, with its sinister, fortress-like cliff formations rises twelve hundred metres above the hilly Catalonian landscape. The name "Montserrat" means "sawn mountain" and is derived by assonance from "Montsagrat", the old designation which the Catalonians substituted for the medieval name "Montsalwatsch". At least as famous in story as the mountain itself, which according to the legend was the site of the fortress of the Holy Grail, is the 9th century monastery, erected just below the tip of the mountain in honour of a miraculous image of the Mother of God.

Valencia. Torreon de Serranos

Valencia, today the third largest city in the country, was formerly capital of the kingdom of the same name. Like most cities in southern Spain it has had an eventful history. Founded originally by Greeks, it came into Carthaginian hands after the First Punic War and later fell to the Romans. In 413 A. D. the Visigoths conquered the Roman "Valentia", which they lost three centuries later to the Arabs who changed the name to "Medîna-bû-tarab", the City of Joy, a name which it still merits today.

The 14th century "Torreon de Serranos", the former northern city gate, has survived almost unaltered and without any essential restoration work having been necessary.

Valencia. The Silk Exchange

Particularly worthy of visit in Valencia is the "Lonja de la Seda", the Silk Exchange, where, on certain fixed days, the silk merchants of the district buy and sell their wares. The beautiful late Gothic building, with the mighty vaulted roof of its hall supported by spiral columns, was erected in the 15th century in the place of a Moorish Alcázar. The decorative details – above all of the doors – are remarkable. Like the numerous gargoyles, they represent the perfection of Gothic ornamentation.

Sagunto

A few kilometres from Valencia, at the foot of a hill on which the famous "Castillo" is built, lies Sagunto. The fortress, whose Iberian designation "Saguntum" gave rise to the present name of the city itself, was the first bulwark conquered by the Carthaginian Hannibal from the Romans after an eight months siege at the beginning of the Second Punic War. When the Romans recovered Sagunto shortly after, they emphasized their now solid hold on the province by new building, including the theatre near the fortress which could accommodate eight thousand spectators.

Punta Ifach

A little off the main road to Alicante in the neighbourhood of the little fishing city of Calpe is the tongue of land Punta Ifach. At the point where the hilly country slopes gently down to the floor of the sea, stone grey walls suddenly rise heavenwards. A gigantic erratic block has found its eternal resting place here exactly on the line where the land meets the sea.

Elche. Palm forest

The Arabs say of the palm-tree that it can only flourish when its foot is in water and its head exposed to the fire of heaven. Both the fiery heaven and the damp earth are present in Elche, a little city between Alicante and Murcia. The tropical climate of this area, which is one of the hottest in southern Spain, is exceptionally favourable to the growth of the palm-trees – they number more than 100,000 – in Elche forest. And if vegetation and climate are already reminders of the proximity of Africa, even more so are the houses on the edge of the forest, quite oriental in style with their flat roofs on which one can sit, their tiny windows and the glaring white colour of their walls.

Purullena

All over Spain, but particularly in the South, are found human settlements where the habitat is prehistoric, but the installations often highly modern. These are the cave-dwellings, sometimes on the edge of cities, sometimes isolated in the otherwise empty countryside. Even today they provide – for gipsies principally, but also for Spaniards – cool and solid shelter.

A View of the Alhambra and Generalife

Granada, the city of southern Spain whose Moorish past has transmitted to our day the most numerous and beautiful memories, was an ancient Iberian foundation. When, in 711 A.D., the year of the landing at Jerez de la Frontera, the Visigoths who then controlled the city were driven out by the Arabs, a period of growth and splendour which was to last for centuries began for Granada. After the fall of the Caliphate of Cordova, "Gharnâta", as the Moors called their Residence, became the spiritual centre of the Arab empire on European soil. At the court of the Nasrides, an Arab tribe which for two centuries and a half provided the royal dynasty, the most famous Arab poets and historians of the day lived and worked. The Alhambra and the Generalife, the two characteristic monuments of Granada, were built in the 14th century, about a hundred years before the expulsion of the Moors from Spain.

Granada, the Alhambra. Court of the Harem (Lion Court)

In the centre of the Alhambra Park on rising ground outside Granada is situated the "Palacio arabe de la Alhambra", built by the Moorish ruler Jusûf I. The bare and monotonous exterior is in sharp contrast with the interior, rich in tasteful detail. Of the three courtyards of the palace, the "Patio de los Leones" bordered by 124 columns and with twelve stone lions around the central fountain, far exceeds in splendour the other two.

Granada. Generalife

Even before the building of the Alhambra had begun, the "Palacio del Generalife" had for decades been serving as summer residence. Whereas in the Alhambra the principal importance was given to the building itself and the gardens are secondary, the Generalife, in keeping with its function as a place of stay for the hot season, shows the opposite tendency. The buildings at the entrance, the courtyard and the royal hall occupy only a small space in contrast to the park which, with its grottoes and artistically-cut hedges offers a beautiful example of Arab garden architecture.

Seville. Alcázar and Cathedral

"He who has not seen Seville has never seen a miracle", says an old Spanish proverb, the truth of which is impressed on the visitor with every day he spends in this old, yet joyfully young city. Seville was founded by the Iberians under the name of "Hispalis" and even in those days was an important inland harbour and entrepôt centre easily reached by ships from the Mediterranean by a passage of about a hundred kilometres up the Guadalquivir. Columbus, when he returned from his voyage of discovery, preferred the sure harbour of Seville to any other, as did innumerable other mariners after him, returning from America with wealth which helped to make the city famous. But even in Moorish times, where it was still called "Ichbilîja", the city was already rich, above all in artistic treasures. Later, in the 14th century, after Ferdinand III had won Seville from the Arabs, it were Moorish architects who built the famous Alcázar. True, the Gothic cathedral, erected a century afterwards, made Seville the poorer by one precious monument, since, for lack of space, a mosque had to be torn down to make way for it. However, the cathedral itself is today considered one of the richest and most splendid Gothic edifices in the world.

Seville. Alcázar and Maidens' Court

The Alcázar of Seville served as Residence for Moorish and, later, Christian rulers. In its present form it was built by Moorish architects in the 14th century on the orders of Peter the Cruel.

Bullfight in Seville

What football is for other Europeans the bullfight is for the Spaniards. With the opening of the season, every Sunday sees vast crowds converging on the "Plaza de Toros" to assist at the age-old encounter between man and bull.

Cordova. Cathedral

Under the Amirate which was established within its walls in the very early days of Moorish rule in Spain, Cordova quickly grew to the rank of an important city. Like Granada at a later date, Cordova was then a cultural centre of Islam to which students came from all over Europe to acquaint themselves with the theses of the Islamic belief. The former Mesquita, the principal Islamic mosque in Europe, became the Catholic cathedral when the Christians occupied Cordova and is today the characteristic monument of the city.

Cordova. Cathedral. Interior

The baffling multiplicity of the 856 columns in the interior of the Mesquita is further intensified by the permanent twilight atmosphere. The building, begun in the 8th century and only finished two hundred years later, underwent transformations in the 16th century which, unfortunately, were not to the advantage of its architectural unity. 63 columns were removed to make room for the erection of a Christian choir.

Madrid.
Puerta del Sol

Madrid, with its 1 700 000 inhabitants, is at once the capital and largest city of Spain. By reason of its central situation, it has always been preferred as the seat of government and, until 1931, the kings of Spain resided here. Today it contains the whole administrative apparatus of national government. It is to these circumstances that Madrid owes its somewhat artificially forced growth, for in itself it seemed predestined, by geography, to an isolated and mediocre existence. Madrid was founded before the 10th century as the small Moorish city and fortress "Madschrît". Even then there was already a "Puerta del Sol", the eastern gate of the city walls, through which one could walk in the direction of the rising sun. Today, the Puerta del Sol is the most important square in the centre of Madrid, since ten of the principal streets branch off from it.

Madrid. Edificio de España

As a city which only began to develop to considerable size in the 19th century, Madrid can naturally show many examples of modern architecture. The "Edificio de España", a skyskraper at the end of the Avenida José Antonio – which is lined down both sides with tall buildings – has become a Madrid landmark. It is 107 metres high and has 3 123 windows and 4 146 doors. In front stands the monument to the poet Cervantes and statues of his two spiritual children, Don Quixote and his servant Sancho Panza whose characters in a certain way incarnate the Spanish soul.

Madrid. The Prado

One of the best-kept and most airy promenades in Madrid is the Prado (meadow). The splendid wide avenue with its numerous gardens is fringed by a series of public buildings, such as the imposing General Post Office, the Navy Ministry and the Navy Museum. A little back from the Prado is the museum of the same name, one of the richest in Europe and containing over 2 500 paintings.

The Escorial

The "Monasterio de San Lorenzo del Escorial", about fifty kilometres northwest of Madrid, was built in the 16th century under Philip II as a summer residence. It contains the tomb of Charles V, father of Philip II, and is modelled on the mighty buildings of the classical Italian style.

Landscape near Toledo and view of the city

The impression of the Middle Ages which Toledo evokes is further heightened by the peculiar character of the neighbouring landscape. Half surrounded by the Tagus, the waters of which lap the city in a great arc, the hill on which Toledo is built rises like a medieval fortress from the surrounding countryside. Long before he enters the city the traveller is struck by its air of proud independence – that independence with which it grew up and which it successfully defended innumerable times.

Toledo. Puerta del Sol

Although Toledo, one of the oldest cities of Spain, shows many Moorish features, such as the confusing network of narrow streets and the almost windowless houses with their cool inner courtyards, its character is determined essentially by Gothic elements. Thus the massive construction of the Puerta del Sol, the exit to the Madrid road, although built in Mudejar style – a mixture of Gothic and Moorish elements – hardly evoke Moorish conceptions of architecture as applied in southern Spain.

Segovia. The Aqueduct

Whereas Madrid itself is poor in relics of the past, its immediate neighbourhood possesses them in surfeit. After Toledo and Escorial, it is Segovia to the Northwest, one of the most picturesque cities of Spain which has preserved the greatest wealth of cultural and historical treasures. Along with medieval monuments, the Roman remains in particular give its character to the city. The aqueduct, over eight hundred metres long, rivals the city walls of Taragona as a great surviving example of Roman building in Spain.

Segovia. Alcázar

The Alcázar of Segovia has two aspects which are in curious contrast to each other. The front, only to be seen when approaching the city from outside, rises like the prow of a small ship into the blue sea of the heavens, while the back, which is reached from the centre of the town, resembles nothing so much, with its air of tranquil assurance, as the broad back of some sturdy old warrior grown hoary in the service of the State.